california: a sketchbook

california a sketchbook

elisha cooper

CHRONICLE BOOKS
SAN FRANCISCO

acknowledgments

Thank you to everyone in this book who let me into their gardens, ranches, boats, and prisons. I appreciate our talks and your time. Thanks to my editor, Alan Rapp, and designer Pamela Geismar, for all the work and for putting up with me. Thanks to everyone at Chronicle. Thank you to Liz Darhansoff and her lake. And thanks to all my friends who helped shape this book into what it is. You know who you are.

Library of Congress Cataloging-in-Publication Data available.
ISBN 0-8118-2697-X

Printed in Hong Kong.

Designed by Pamela Geismar.

Distributed in Canada by
Raincoast Books
8680 Cambie Street
Vancouver, British Columbia V6P 6M9

10 9 8 7 6 5 4 3 2 1

Chronicle Books
85 Second Street
San Francisco, California 94105

www.chroniclebooks.com

for elise

map of contents

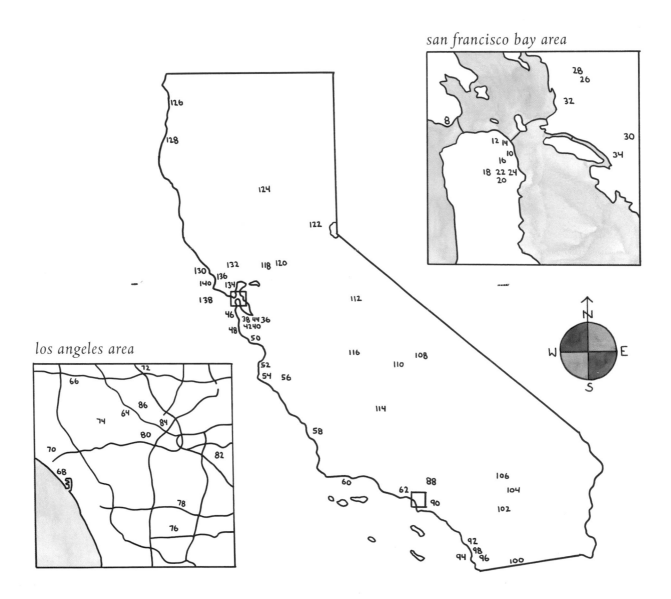

san francisco bay area

los angeles area

golden gate bridge

California begins for me looking out at San Francisco Bay. From the Marin side, grass hills tumble down past windswept trees to crashing water and the edge of the Pacific. It's a good place for a beginning, a hopeful place. Beyond the water is the span of the bridge and beyond the bridge are the cream-colored buildings of San Francisco. I cross – past the place where people jump, past tourists taking pictures, past one singing toll worker – into the city.

caffe centro

"So intimidating!" says Gabrielle Fisher of the Caffe Centro espresso machine. "You have to keep everything going at once!" Fisher is confiding in me about the dangers of the job. A customer in lime green pants orders a single decaf latte. Fisher clicks grounds, pats them flat, fires the espresso drip, pours milk from the pitcher into the cup and then, carefully, rolls the foam. "The foam machine is the most scary part. Makes a lot of noise," she says. People in snazzy eyewear and neatly trimmed facial hair wait in line. When not serving espresso, Fisher gardens, volunteers, goes to a lot of movies. She moved from back east and graduated a few years ago – who knows what's next. At the end of her shift she pedals off on her bike.

12 *chinatown, san francisco*

Nora Wong is to my right. Mable Gee is across from me. Helen Wu is to my left. I look over Lilly Poon's shoulder as the deal moves from north to east to south to west. Tiles with engravings of bamboo, circles, and flowers are tossed down and stacked up to a backdrop of laughter and raised eyebrows. Talk flows from English (to tell me the rules) to Chinese (when they're serious). When someone wins, the other three reluctantly pass chips pulled from drawers in the table. It's two dollars a hand. We talk about politics, luck, a past trip to the Great Wall. Poon tells me about the badminton club she started sixty-one years ago. Wu brings me coffee. Hours pass – the "click, click" of play broken only by the rattle of reshuffling and the occasional comment: "Everybody's got a good hand. Except you!"

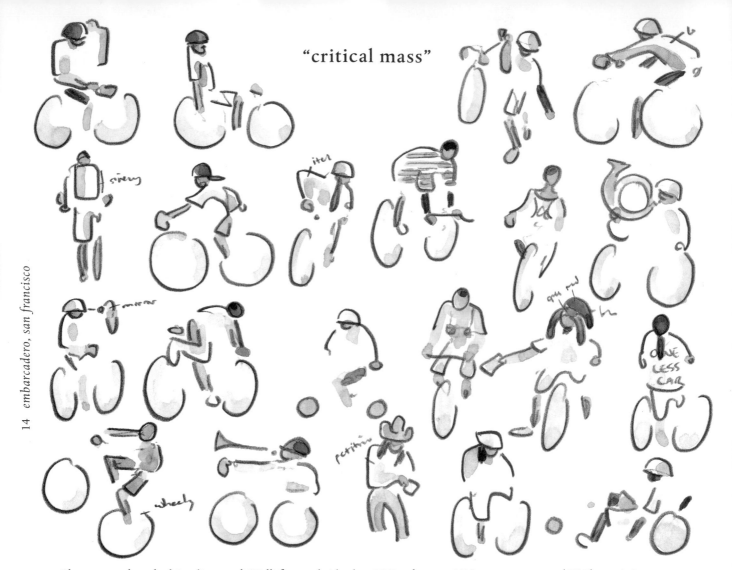

"critical mass"

Flyers passed out by bicyclists read: "Talk fast and ride slow." "One less car." "Not one more road." "Clean air."
"We are traffic." Petitions also circle among the crowd of bicyclists, as does one megaphone. Then, after

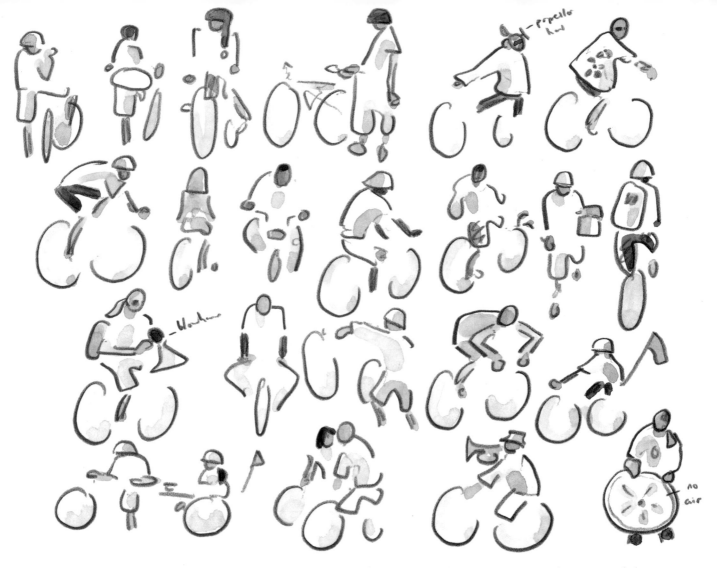

debating where to ride, the monthly rally takes to the streets, confronts motorists, and ties up rush hour traffic. I pedal along behind. A rider in front of me blows bubbles that float down onto everyone around him.

slim's

Eleven o'clock on Saturday night and hometown band Box Set is tangled up in cords. Jim Brunberg, lead singer, tries to avoid electrical wires and adjust amps and repair strings and play a mandolin and sing the song all at the same time (he announces between songs that they're looking for a guitar tech). The good-looking Brunberg starts to sweat through his T-shirt; the other singer with the pigtails spends a lot of time with a towel. But when the wires work and the harmony is right the crowd sways and sings along. The band plays their hit. Then they play, according to Brunberg, "some new songs along with other noises." One's a love song about a bed. A cute girl on my left mouths along to the song and gives Brunberg a knowing wave.

castro theater

Outside the San Francisco International Lesbian & Gay Film Festival there is the cheek kiss, the double-cheek kiss, the bear hug, the whack-the-back hug, the don't-spill-my-coffee hug, the get-off-your-damn-cell-phone hug, the laugh-from-behind-when-the-huggee-doesn't-know-who-it-is hug, the just-give-me-my-ticket-and-that's-the-only-contact-you're-getting hug, the kick-one-leg-out-for-no-apparent-reason hug, the eyes-closed-rock-back-and-forth hug, the love-handle-pat hug, the fix-the-huggee's-hair hug, the check-out-someone-over-the-shoulder hug, the one-minute hug, the one-second hug, the look-around-for-the-next-hug hug, the wave. So many options and the movie's about to start.

Juan Carlos points out the brains. They're a bit mushy and used to be in a cow. He also shows me the hog snouts, chicken feet, oxtails, intestines, tripe, and gizzards that line the cool, well-stocked counter of the *carnicería,* and describes for me what dishes and soups each are used for. There's a sign for *huevos*

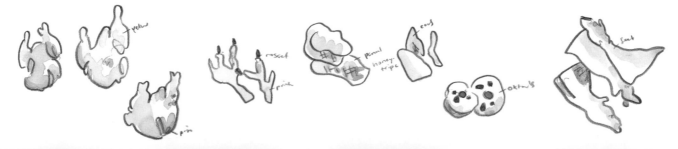

de toros ($1.99 lb), but he's all out. It's a specialty, very popular, and he won't have any more until next week when the supplier kills another bull. Why eat bovine testicles? Carlos gives me a smile, flexes his right forearm across his chest, and says, "Power!"

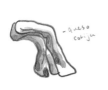

kqed public radio

his mike is
color of
her hair

monitor

Behind the soundproof door of Studio A the call-in show *Forum* sounds off. Host Michael Krasny guides guests and their comments (about a state senate race, a new ballpark), takes notes behind a gray mustache, juggles contentious connections with a careful voice: "Jeff, forgive me, but you've brought up a spate

shifting

of topics!" Across from him, behind glass, producer Holly Kernan hops around an editing room lined with bulletins from *All Things Considered* and cassettes labeled *Fresh Air*. Phone lines light up, Kernan answers, sees what Anthony from

Richmond has to say, types it into a monitor that relays the particulars to Krasny. She whispers words into the mike that go to his ear then out his mouth. Then she signals him with a pen over the rising guitar music countdown to break (brought to you in part by a new fruit juice).

vermont & 18th streets

Billboards everywhere. Ads for Gap, Banana Republic, Dockers, Levi's, Jamba Juice, Diet Coke, Coke, *The Bay Guardian*, Chevy cars, Ford trucks, Apple computers, VW bugs, whiskey, vodka, beer, insurance, health care. There are so many billboards

in the city that the San Francisco Planning Commission doesn't keep track: layers of ads, ads painted on buildings, ads painted over on buildings. Up on one billboard, a worker painting a new ad dangles back and forth on a rope.

university of california, berkeley

A shirtless man walks down the Telegraph Avenue sidewalk on his hands. A man waits for the WALK sign then dances into the street and waves the Torah. A vendor sells *I'd Rather Be Smashing Imperialism* bumper stickers outside the record store. A protester ties himself to the top of the Campanile for a week. At the salad place I overhear a girl tell a story about a guy who, when he comes into town, puts traffic cones on the hood of her car: "He says he's marking his territory, like he owns me or something!" She goes on: "He's been doing this for months and now I have like twenty cones in my closet."

chez panisse

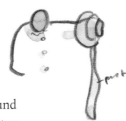

The kitchen bustles in preparation for lunch. Chefs swirl around wooden cutting boards and under hanging copper pots. I try to stay out of the way. Prosciutto is sliced for appetizers (the hogs are from Oregon and fed on hazelnuts). Sous-chef Jennifer Johnson works on artichoke ravioli. She fills, folds, and pastes as another chef threads five-foot-long sheets of pasta through a pasta roller. Chefs banter: "We should probably start on the eggplants." Chefs sing. They talk about color. They talk about taste. They taste. They add. Johnson lays out a plate of ravioli and when chefs walk by they spoon a bite. Salmon's sliced. Parsley's cut. Garlic's peeled. Smells appear, then recede, replaced by something stronger. A chef removes bad blackberries from a dessert plate of peaches. On one wall is a memo: "Some people are still using water from the espresso machines for tea, etc. . . . thinking [it's] okay. It isn't. Don't use espresso-machine water. Please."

mayor jerry brown

Mayor Jerry Brown, at the early morning clergy breakfast, on the state of the world: "The message, the interpretation, is out of whack!"

Mayor Brown on learning:
"All people, all mammals, can learn."

Mayor Brown on ownership:
"Children belong to themselves."

Mayor Brown on difficulties: "Probably the most difficult thing anybody has to do is descending the birth canal!"

Mayor Brown on change: "It's no time to cool off. It's no time for the 'intoxicating drug of gradualism.'"

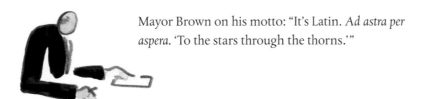

Mayor Brown on his motto: "It's Latin. *Ad astra per aspera.* 'To the stars through the thorns.'"

Mayor Brown on problems: "There's a lot of problems. I want to work on them all!"

Mayor Brown on being thanked for coming: "Thank *you.* I'm energized!"

destiny arts center

Some kids practice their martial arts forms (the dragon, the long cat, the medium cat, the twisted horse, the reverse glass horse, the star). Other kids practice their martial arts forms on each other. A girl in pigtails knocks a barrette out of another girl's hair. A boy adjusting his belt during the middle of sparring gets kicked in the gut. A girl falls hard on her rear – and gets up. These are cool kids. Kate Hobbs, instructor and director, reminds them of the fundamentals: "It's time to put in your mouthguard," and "After you hit 'em, remember to bow!" Near the door is a flyer for an upcoming class: *Introduction to the Kajunkenbo Punch Attack.*

oakland raiders

Tim Brown believes. At the end of another loss on a drive that won't change anything, Brown dives for

the ball, coming up with a small gain and a grass stain. Distractions don't seem to matter: cheerleaders

who beam up into emptying stands, face-painters who can't find their way out, hangers-on who crowd the sidelines, an organization that just can't win. All those peel away and it's just a game on a field with

a ball. A minute left, fourth down. Brown holds hands with his linemen in the huddle, then breaks to

the back of the end zone and jumps high to catch the ball for a touchdown. Taking off his helmet, he can

only watch as the game ends. When he leaves the field he hugs the guy who covered him all day.

coyote creek & el jardin community gardens

Chuòng Nguyen's skin looks more parched than his soil. His lush garden has six children's wading pools brimming with water and celery. The rest of the Coyote Creek community garden is packed with bamboo markers, hose bibs, wheelbarrows, vegetables. Across town, the El Jardin community garden looks much the same: a tool-strewn green landscape of twenty-by-thirty-foot plots, used mostly by refugees and recent immigrants. At the nearby Dúc Viên Buddhist Community Pagoda garden I watch Viên Ngũ as she waters plants by hand. Under a tent on the edge of the plot I'm given a lunch of rice, bean sprouts, basil (red and green), and mint. Dishes are washed and placed on racks in the sun to dry.

stanford university

38 palo alto

At first I mistake Stanford for a corporate headquarters. The campus is full of serene buildings, clipped lawns, quiet (you can almost smell the endowment, the government grants). At a volleyball game on the green lawn, ergonomically correct recumbent bicycles glide by. The players keep up a constant chatter: "Yours!" "Get that!" "I'd call a net on you but I won't." "That was stupid, plain and simple." "Can you do me a favor and not hit too hard. I have a bad wrist."

emerald bay distributor

"They're glad to see the water guy," says Tom Bitter. "We're bringing them something they want." Bitter is talking behind the big wheel of his truck. We pull up at office complexes, he jumps out, loads two forty-seven-pound water bottles on his shoulders, walks past secretaries and cubicles to the cooler in the back where he drops off fulls and picks up empties. Between drops Bitter tells me stories: the time someone put a goldfish in the cooler, the exercise studio with the mean poodle, customers who just

all water cans
from on plane:
hitch. hershy

don't understand. "People say, 'We're out of water! Get out here now, or else!' and they don't realize they're not the only one." Bitter marvels at the new wealth made by the people he delivers to. He's looking to change jobs. At one stop he has to remove a spider from the cooler, then try to explain how it got there. When he comes out he gets in his truck, rolls down the window, and spits.

yahoo!

Purple walls, yellow trim. Yellow walls, purple trim. Purple couches. Purple conference tables. Purple stools in the espresso bar. *Not* in the Internet company's colors are brand marketer Julie Beddome's toes, painted metallic. I look at them as she strides past cubicles. On the sides of cubicles are Yahoo! beach towels. In a glass case are Yahoo! hats and Yahoo! slinkies. One of Beddome's jobs is product placement: getting Yahoo! on TV, in movies, everywhere. When she walks me out she gives me a Yahoo! Frisbee, Yahoo! T-shirt, and Yahoo! water bottle – all in a yellow Yahoo! sand bucket. In the parking lot (where the curbs are purple) Beddome points out two colleagues pulling up in sports cars bought with cashed-out stock. Beddome shows me her '64 Ford Fairlane. The company is paying to shrink-wrap it purple, with racing flames and Yahoo! written on the sides.

iHarvest

David Wadhwani, cofounder of iHarvest, greets me in his socks. He's not the only one. Of the seven workers at the Silicon Valley start-up, two others wear socks, one wears sandals, three are barefoot. The stuffed frog on top of one computer wears nothing at all. Wadhwani pads back and forth on the suite's new carpet past windows that still have price tags. He looks over shoulders, quietly cajoling and helping coworkers as screens flicker and change to the soft tap of keys. A fridge hums gently behind him. Contents: cereal, diet soda, mayonnaise, cold pasta, hot fudge, salad dressing, blow pops, filtered water. In another room are two foldout cots. When The Product comes out, they're going to take over the world.

iharvest

pink

white

fountain at
node women with
water coming out of
clothes washer

marble

maverick's

"The waves are hungry today," growls the open-shirted onlooker. We're watching the water and he's telling me a story about the guy whose board broke in two a week back. Three surfers walk past us and launch their boards. They push out, ducking under low rollers, rising over white foam, paddling out to where the monsters pound a quarter-

mile away. Even from that distance the waves look massive. They take their time falling, and when they do it knots my stomach. The three surfers are now specks, bobbing specks (maybe they should be called bobbers, not surfers), passing in and out of my vision. Then, I can't see them at all.

On the dunes there's a lot going on. Elephant seal mothers give birth and seagulls swoop down to clean up placentas. Males fight, slam into each other's necks, and chase losers out to sea. Females are mounted by males who run over babies in their haste. Babies, or weaners, nurse from mothers and gain around three hundred pounds in a month. Super-weaners trick two mothers into feeding them and get even bigger. Dead weaners venture out among sharks that swim past the break. While walking back from the dunes I'm startled by one elephant seal lumbering along the path toward me, with a park aid waving his arms and herding from behind.

año nuevo state reserve

50 santa cruz

Young girls in old cars cruise the Avenue. They get out and hang in spaghetti-strap tank tops, show their belly buttons, wait for the late movie, maybe dip into the coffee shop for an iced latte (skim milk). As evening falls and the temperature drops the girls move closer together, bumping into each other, arms tucked tight under elbows. After a while I realize – these girls are *freezing*. But they don't go for the sweaters tied around their hips.

Stapled to the cypress tree is this public notice: "Notice of a minor and trivial amendment to a combined development permit . . . unless objections are received, the amendment will be granted to allow for installation of artificial artistic rock to cover existing rip rap retention structures on the coastal bluffs of the golf course greens (Fairways 16 & 17) of the Cypress Point Club." The result, according to the Planning & Building Inspection Department, will create "a molded-bluff face with the appearance of cracks to blend with the adjacent natural bluff face." Down on the (natural) water I watch otters who, if they swim a bit farther in, will be trespassing on private property.

The Big Sur International Marathon is torture. Runners have six uphills (one almost two miles long), seven downhills (not any easier), heat, head winds, cross winds, very cross winds, breathtaking views that mock every step; leg cramps, stomach cramps, sunburned shoulders, chafing armpits, bent toenails, blistering toes, bleeding nipples. And, at mile twenty-four the runners have to deal with bagpipers. Luckily, when it's all over, they can walk to an airy tent for a free massage.

big sur international marathon

neil bassetti farms

broccoli

metallic gr—

bro—

yellow

hi tech water pump

"Worms and mildew get kind of boring after a while, but there's some stuff that makes you check your books," says Patrick Barbree, pest control advisor. He slices heads of lettuce, checks for bugs, tells me about *lepidopterous* larvae. Barbree's in charge of miles of cabbage, cauliflower, and broccoli. We walk in a circular stop-and-go route through the rows, his truck idling behind us. "That's a bad guy," he shrugs, holding up then

neck

check
rows

handing me a corn earworm. If the situation deteriorates Barbree gets on his cell phone and calls in a crop duster. Agriculture in the Salinas Valley is *the* business, with soil people, fertilizer guys, water men (and upper and lower valley continually squabbling over the aquifer). As Barbree hacks more heads he mentions that he can take all the fresh vegetables he wants. But, he adds, "I'm a major beef eater."

The early morning Mass at the mission is calm and cool, with eleven parishioners sitting in pews and thumbing their rosaries. I go to local Cuesta College, where, in front of a packed auditorium, master hypnotist Christine Michele is putting people to sleep. "This will be a very pleasant, enjoyable experience for you!" she exhorts. She commands the hypnotees to raise their arms. "Lifting and rising, the higher it gets the better you feel, the better you feel, the higher it gets!" Hands rise, chins drop. "Everything I say becomes the absolute truth the instant I say it!"

exxon

pelicans look prehistoric, as if they'd lost forever

To visit an oil rig I contact the people at Exxon headquarters in Houston. The people at headquarters contact their people in California. The people in California set up a meeting. The people in California check with other people at headquarters back in Houston (their people's people's people). I'm told I can't go. There's a lot of publicity surrounding the anniversary of the Exxon Valdez oil spill in Alaska and it's not a good time right now for the company (they suggest a visit to another company's rigs). I head to the shore anyway. Not far from Exxon's Los Flores Canyon Oil & Gas Processing Plant is a field of beautiful pink flowers. Out on the water pelicans glide over rolling waves. And in the distance stands one of Exxon's oil rigs, named Harmony.

calle del barco development

Chris Dean, Malibu town geologist, has great maps. They're blue and crinkly and rippled with topographic lines. He shows them to me and talks about the land. "So, we have a potentially active fault, we have steep slopes, weak rock in a lot of points, and that adds up to a lot of problems." Factor in over-watered lawns and a history of private sewage drainage, and it only gets worse. The result: mud slides.

We get into his 4 x 4, drive to a slide in the hills, walk around. Dean uses words like *scarp* and *toe* and *landshear.* "The land down here was up near the scarp up there." He gestures at sandbags, and the hydraugers that puncture and drain the hillside. We watch the land stay still for the moment, then drive back down the hill past a solitary chimney from the recent fire. Chris Dean does not live in Malibu.

ymca gym

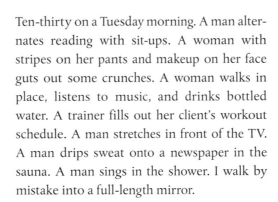

Ten-thirty on a Tuesday morning. A man alternates reading with sit-ups. A woman with stripes on her pants and makeup on her face guts out some crunches. A woman walks in place, listens to music, and drinks bottled water. A trainer fills out her client's workout schedule. A man stretches in front of the TV. A man drips sweat onto a newspaper in the sauna. A man sings in the shower. I walk by mistake into a full-length mirror.

cameron thor studio

Guys with perfect chins and girls in breast-hugging shirts (actors) work on scenes while Cameron Thor, acting coach, tries to sit still. He can't. He leaps onstage and whispers advice in an actor's ear. He directs: "Go 'Ahhh!' No! To her!" He encourages: "You must win this woman!" One actor crawls across the floor in lingerie, bawling. Thor slaps his thigh, laughing: "Yes!" He shouts for his assistant, gives him a fifty

dollar bill to run out and buy a CD with a song that will prove a point. He pats himself on the back. He gives actors notes: "Have a feeling, change it!" He congratulates: "That was a slice of heaven!" He interrupts himself with anecdotes and advice: "I once hit [famous actor] with a phone book to try to get him to relax!" For three hours he keeps this up. The best actor in the studio is Cameron Thor.

Give-and-take on the basketball courts: "No, no, no." "Yeah, yeah, yeah!" "One of ya'll touch the ball." "Offa ya." "What?" "Boolsh∗∗." "Brick." "Bound." "Foul." "FOUL?!" "All ball!" "He swatted that sh∗∗ away!" "Don't even deny it." "I got wheels, man!" "Garbage." "That sh∗∗ was a gift." "We here to make you feel better." "What's the score?" "Eight-up." "We're up by two." "PASS THE BALL!" "Wooo!" "Lucky mutha." "I made that shot under duress!" "It's all good." "Game." "All day." "Next!"

frank gehry house

It's a weird house, with metal sheeting, jutting wire fencing, and odd-shaped windows wrapped around an old pink wooden two-story. It's a cool house, designed years ago and lived in now by Frank Gehry, architect. The street numbers near the front door look like they've been removed to discourage visitors (people like me). I call his offices to ask about the house and contact Berta Gehry, his wife. Her favorite details are the windows and the skylights. What she likes least are people ringing the doorbell to ask if they can come in for a tour. There have been all sorts of strange reactions to the house from neighbors. It's no wonder that the Gehrys are leaving tomorrow on a trip to Europe.

fence-like material from Santa Monica Fence Co.

funk doobiest & byze

Listen up. This is the studio. This is Funk Doobiest at the studio, rapping into the mike, then jumping up on a table and dancing, arms wide, palms flat.

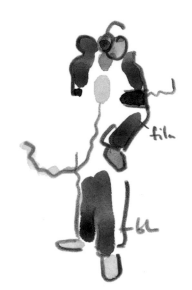

This is Funk Doobiest on air: "Yo, Eli! Whattup! Sh**. Aw, sh**" That was Funk Doobiest's producer hitting the seven-second delay to censor the word.

Back at rap label Priority Records, Byze, West Coast promoter who set up the session with Funk Doobiest, nurses a sore throat with hot tea, points out the framed platinum records on the wall for Ice Cube, says how one album "dropped" 300,000 records in a week.

A coworker comes by with a child and Byze mentions the last time he baby-sat for her. Then Byze says goodbye: Peace.

the ivy

flowers

valet parking · big cars

hunched

slow

listns

what's for lunc

After a fifteen-minute wait, Lynn Pleshette, agent, has had enough. We storm out of the Ivy. "Insulting!" she exclaims, and we walk down the block to Orso. Pleshette settles into a corner table. "Much better crowd," she mutters. We're in a prime spot – the regular table of the producer of a recent hit. I order chilled tomato soup, then grilled tuna with braised fennel, white beans and spinach with roasted red pepper butter (or something). Pleshette is having trouble with her cell phone. Diners move back and forth from their tables, visiting here, congratulating there. Pleshette points out who's who. One woman comes over and the conversation goes like this: "You in the same house?" "Yeah!" "So are we!" "Yeah?" "Cool. I'll try to walk back to my table in these heels."

tibby elementary school

Ms. Antunez – or Beth Antunez as she might be known outside of school – is teaching math to her third-grade class in room 101. Hands rise or touch Ms. Antunez's pant leg. Students whisper and help each other. Some students quietly wiggle and squirm (not many feet are on the floor). Uniforms come undone. Occasionally Ms. Antunez reminds a student why they're here:

"Alejandro, work!" And then there's that wonderful moment when I think I see from students' faces that a fact becomes clear. They rush to the board and chalk up answers. On one wall are English lessons: "The fish went into Lucia's hair." "All of the fish in the river loved Lucia." "Lucia went to live in a cave with the fish, the river, and an iguana."

"Braids is artwork . . . art in the hair." Hana RaNu,El peers over her glasses and gives me a smile to see if I'm getting it. In her soothing voice she adds, "The joy of braids, you don't have to do nothing with it. Just live." RaNu,El herself has designer locks, beautiful small blond coils. "Locks for life," she croons. RaNu,El pulls the hair tight on the braidee's head, tucks hard. She can add extensions – plastic or real –

put in Nubian knots or a Senegalese twist. Sometimes she ties a cowrie shell into the braid, her personal touch. "They look cultural and cute, don't they?" I ask if she can braid my short hair and she laughs and laughs. I go to Watts Towers, which look like heads with braids piled high.

hannam supermarket & naga food market

The Hannam Supermarket on Olympic Boulevard has gobo, mango, ketyp, pickle, nila, lobok, gingerroot, altari radish, kabocha squash, sweet yam, cabbage, kale. The nearby Naga Food Market has lapu lapu cabrilla, bisugo, dalagang bukid, phil gulunggong, catfish, red rock cod, baby juma, sheephead bacoco, squid, and Lina Sarmento, the manager, who's worried that I'm drawing her fish for the competition.

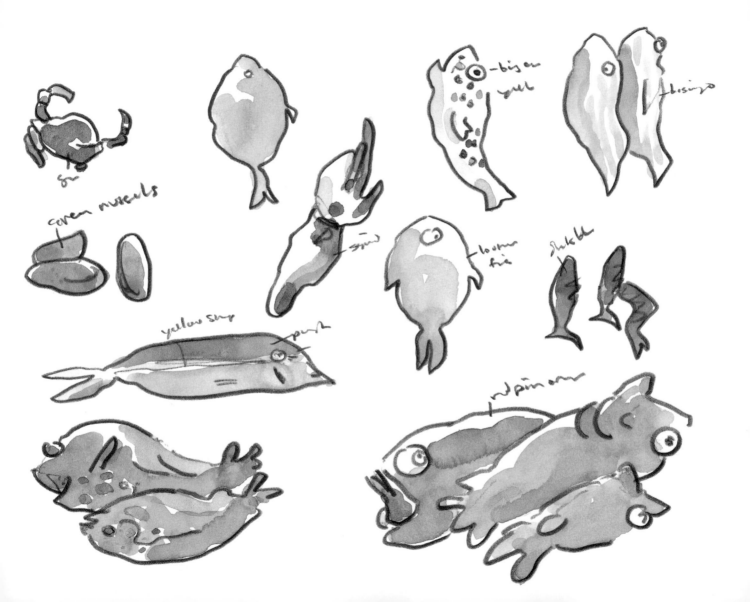

soundset car stereo and accessories

Humberto Galvan has a nice smile, which I can't see right now because he's upside down in the trunk of a car. He's telling me about his family, how his mother came from Mexico with six kids when his father died, how he wasn't very good at school but loved music and cars, which led him to where he is now, owning the shop, installing stereos, and tinting windows. The rear window, the one he's working on, is the hardest. Galvan takes his time. He separates plastic sheets with his teeth, squirts solvent, smoothes air bubbles, splices with a razor. "You have to have a steady hand," I hear him say. "It's like surgery, eh?" Galvan works with his brother and cousin. Nephews help out, friends are customers. While we're talking, a truck runs into a car on the street and everyone rushes outside to see what's up but Galvan keeps working.

lotus festival

stretching

joyous drums

flailing

purple

green

Backstage, the Yoki Daiko Japanese Taiko Drum Troupe gets dressed. They peel out of blue jeans and baseball hats and slip into *happi* robes and sashes. They stretch, give back rubs, practice soundlessly without sticks. When they hit the stage

and the first drumbeat drops, the crowd stops and sucks in its breath. Even the motion away from the drums has sound. The troupe flails in unison, then takes solo turns on the big drum, legs wide apart. The drums rumble. The rhythm's contagious.

el contento & alcyona drives

A helicopter buzzes overhead – following traffic, a developing accident, a piece of news, anything. A second helicopter flies by. Over thirty police helicopters, fire helicopters, traffic helicopters, and news helicopters operate in the metropolitan area – and that's not counting private helicopters. A third helicopter flies over. Other sounds line up and take their turns: a doorbell, a phone, the whoosh of a sports utility vehicle making the turns, the beep of a delivery truck backing up, an answering machine, an alarm.

house of dreams rave

At five in the afternoon I call the number. At six I drive to the place with the tickets. At ten I go to the place that has the map, but it's moved, and at twelve I go to the new location. At one – now it's morning and I'm full of caffeine – I drive up curving anonymous roads, and at two I reach the mountaintop

and the House of Dreams Rave. At three I dance to Jungle. At four I dance to Trance. At five I've lost track counting how many girls are sucking on lollipops, lost track of how many times I'm asked what drug I'm on. At six the sun comes up. At seven the rave ends. At eight, coming down the mountain, I drive past the accident site where two cars drove off the road.

fairhaven memorial park & mortuary

"Basically, there's your prepping and your services . . . you have above ground, you have regular ground, you have lawn crypts, you have niches, you have a depository." Tiffany Bright is giving me the rundown at Fairhaven Memorial Park & Mortuary – the place that contains the remains of the man who built retirement community Leisure World. At Fairhaven, you can get a $16,000 gold-plated casket with a burgundy velvet interior. You can have a horse-drawn hearse. You can definitely have flowers. Bright's favorite are pink roses and when her time comes she's planning on a "full-blown traditional service, cherry casket, Dixieland band. I want a party!" The bathroom on the way to the Garden of Serenity has a box of tissues resting on the urinal.

legoland

directed to truck

shades

Security is tight and it's understandable. A few days ago a woman sent her son over the fence to rip Legos off the big red L that sits on the side of Lego Drive. Jim Delmer, security guard, talks with me about this and other perils of the job outside his guardhouse (not made of Legos). "To be honest with you, a security guy is a baby-sitter for adults," he says. Delmer has a crew cut and a square chin; Legoland needs men like him to protect Mini-Land. Legoland is building and Delmer waves through trucks with boxes. Some boxes have Lego giraffes and alligators. Says Delmer, "Every once in a while I'll be doing a foot patrol at night and I'll get startled by – I'm not an edgy guy, you know – a life-size [Lego] person. I thought for a second, you know, it was a guy. Same thing happened with a wildebeest."

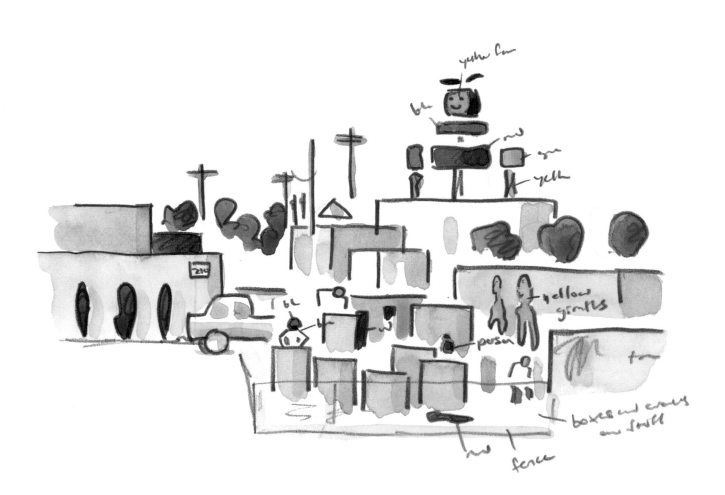

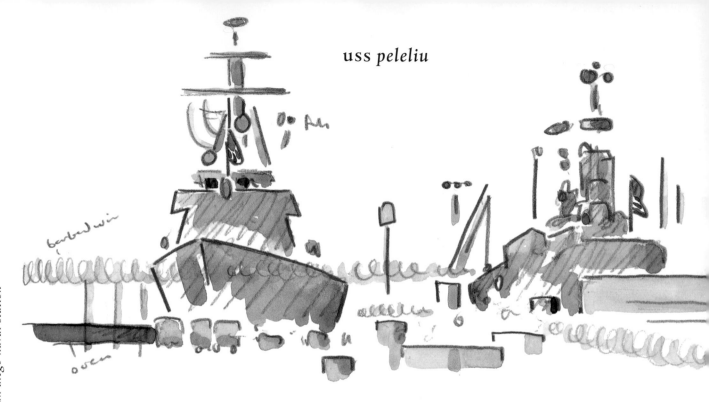

uss *peleliu*

From the bridge of the USS *Peleliu* there's nothing but ocean. We're cruising at eighteen knots on latitude 31°2', twenty miles off the coast (a hovercraft brings me out). I listen to Capt. Gary R. Jones and talk with the kids who chart the ship's course. If there's a problem in the world the *Peleliu* is there, with jets and two thousand marines. Below in the mess there's hot dogs and mashed potatoes. In the officers' dining room we eat lasagna and broccoli. Three officers take me on a tour. We scramble up ladders, visit the CIC, CSMC (the officers use a lot of abbreviations). We go on deck where two men jog. We scramble down ladders, visit the ship's laundry, post office, sleeping berths, walk-in refrigerator (boxes and boxes of margarine). The ship can be gone six months. There's a bakery on board. A cook scripts icing on a cake: *Congratulations on your Re-enlistment MA 1 (SW) Rodriguez.*

cranes

different colors for different jobs

white glove

coil

captain

cuffs

collar

fashion valley mall

Items I don't buy at the Fashion Valley Mall: a pair of ultrasheer control top leggings, an Oscar de La Renta 36B purple bra, a size 3 Nearly-Me Breast Enhancer, an assortment of eau de toilette, lip lacquer, toning mist, exfoliant, and pink-glow eyeshadow, a silver eyelash curler, a tiger skin skirt, a leopard skin skirt, a rose cashmere turtleneck, a dress with "Bon Appetit" written on it in curvy letters, a Paloma Picasso purse, a pair of Versace shades, an ostrich-feather hat, a Prada bag, and a pair of Manolo Blahnik tellaroplai pumps.

Alfredo Castillejo is a gardener. He cuts lawns five days a week and makes sixty dollars a day. He's done this for eight years. He has a soft voice, a whisper of a mustache, a scruff of a goatee. He has sagging pants stained with grass cuttings and sweat, weighed down by clippers in the back pocket. I come along as he roars into still neighborhoods in his pickup. Castillejo says it's nice working outside but there are drawbacks. "When they have many things for trimming

and they have stones it's terrible to work in that." A woman emerges from the house across the road. "Terrible!" she says, addressing me and pointing at his gas-powered leaf blower. "They were outlawed. But they still keep doing it. I mean, look at that! . . . It's all these Mexican gardeners that do this and it's not very good." She tells him, leaves. Castillejo shrugs, "Some are good. Some are no good." After this we talk *fútbol*; his team is Atlético Morelia.

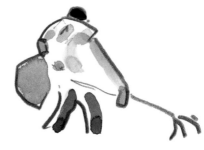

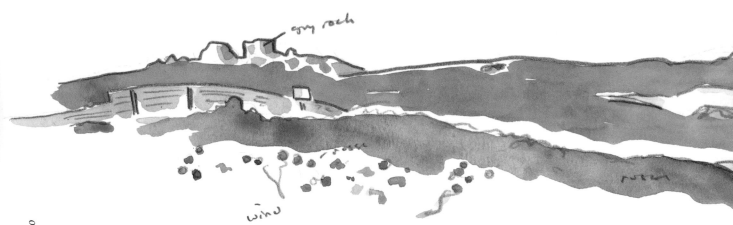

Three miles from the fence, over unforgiving terrain, is a tree. In its shade are four men who just crossed. I give them my water (they ran out an hour ago); they offer me a smoke. They're undocumented, were visiting family and are returning to their jobs. Three are gardeners in L.A. One is a cook. One has gold-capped teeth and sits on a rusted toy tractor and jokes that he's going to ride it all the way to L.A. A border patrol helicopter flies overhead and we don't talk for a bit. They tell me their hopes for good jobs, and right now, for a beer. There's a three-hour hike ahead, then a phone call and a ride. They ask my name and give me theirs. One man says that before he leaves he's stopping at the church on the horizon.

palm springs bowl

Where are the people? They're not on Palm Canyon Drive, where you can smell the blacktop melt. They're not on the sidewalks whose hidden fountains erupt every minute. They're not in the shops or restaurants that spray mist and they're not at the public outdoor pool where I go for a swim. I find them bowling. Bowling in the cool cool air-conditioning of Palm Springs Bowl. It's league night and everyone is here. Men and women in striped wide-collared shirts skip, slide, and twirl, then lean to coax the ball away from the gutter. Returns rumble. A man polishes his ball. If anyone goes outside for a smoke they come back quick.

joshua tree national park

Nothing moves. Round boulders and scraggly trees (*Yucca brevifolia*) stand still. The temperature sits above a hundred. Then things start to change. Shadows creep over rocks, slink along crevices, roll over climbers, leap to the next outcrop. They crawl up the trees (*humwichawa* or *hunuvat chiy'a* as called by the

local Cahuilla tribe), leaving the prickly tops touched in gold. If I look away for a moment they gain an inch. The boulders (*monzogranite*) change color from ocher to pink to russet to blue to gray and the temperature cools fast.

excavation site EA-1

"Yumba" is what you yell when you find something special. Sort of like calling "yahtzee." But, says archaeology professor Matt Hall, "you get in trouble if you yell 'Yumba' and the crew decides it's not a yumba." This time it is: two arrowheads. Hall's students mark artifacts with pin-flags. The ground's marked with shrapnel and tank tracks; the site's on a marine base and we're told not to touch any unexploded ordnance (bombs). At lunch the crew sometimes have pin-flag javelin contests. Today they

tell stories about their best finds. Professor Hall talks about how an expedition he was on in Egypt found the Sphinx's nose. Everyone gets a big laugh out of that one. After lunch they grid the site, tell jokes from *The Simpsons*. When we drive out at the end of the day the archaeologists play a trivia game by walkie-talkie: "What's the state flower of California?" "The golden poppy?" "Excellent!"

manzanar japanese internment camp national monument

The camp is almost not here. Foundations stretch through the scrub, barely showing what used to be. Ross R. Hopkins, superintendent for the national monument, sits in his prefab office and we talk about the 10,000 Japanese-Americans kept here behind barbed wire during World War II. Hopkins majored in history at Northwestern. He has a light blue '68 Jeep, a bandage on his left thumb. He tells me about one relocated girl who, after a month at the camp, told her mother she didn't like Japan and wanted to

go back to California. He tells me about the battalion of men who fought in Europe, the group that broke code in the Pacific. There are a lot of stories and Hopkins is working on an oral history. Some locals and veterans don't like the monument; Hopkins gets threats and his home phone is unlisted. As I leave, Hopkins remarks that we like to think of ourselves as tolerant but that stops cold when we get outside our own group: "People spoke up, but damn few."

sequoia national park

Jay Snow is walking across America and has gotten this far. When he started over a year ago he was "real cynical and bitter" but things got better. At every mountain pass he yodels ("I'm a yodeler!"). I ask for an example and he gives it. He also takes off all his clothes at each peak and I take him on his word. He's gone through six pairs of boots. His parents send noodles through the mail; he writes back and the letter is a column for his hometown paper in Oklahoma. Why stop in Sequoia? "The trees, I suppose." It's also a "place

you can get your head together." A woman he met on the trail is coming to visit. The generosity of people he's met has been unbelievable. He lets me in on his philosophy: "You get what you give." He has a happily lined face, three children living in Europe and elsewhere. We look over a map and chart his path straight into the Pacific. But, he says, "I'm never going to stop walking, that's just the way it's going to be."

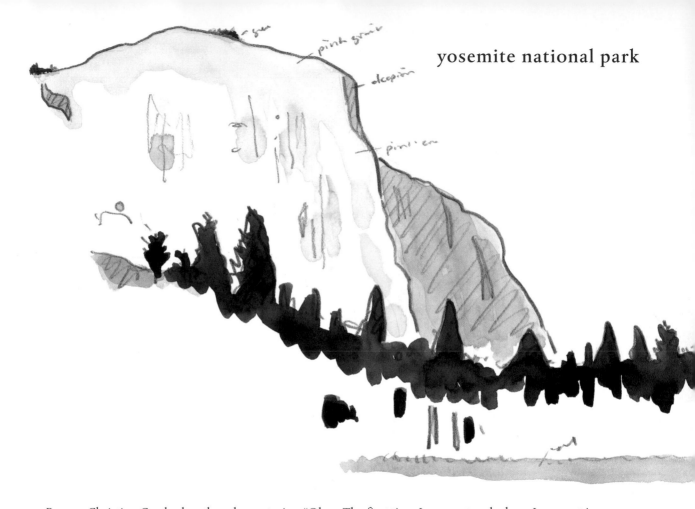

yosemite national park

Ranger Christine Cowles has three bear stories: "Okay. The first time I encountered a bear I was out in the backcountry.... I saw something across a meadow. I thought, dear God, there's a bear and he's going to eat me. I panicked, couldn't sleep all night, and I'm telling myself, 'But I'm a ranger!' ... The second time I dealt with a bear was, let's see, I can't remember that one.... Another time I saw a bear, out in the backcountry again. Night camp, finished eating, boiling water, bottle of wine. Heard something in the

bushes. Because it was so dark I turned on my flashlight, and I caught the light of his eyes and he was this close [she reaches out and touches me]. But this time I know something changed in me, because I'd been working with the wildlife people here and I knew he's not here to hurt me, he's just looking for food. He was much more my friend. So this time I was like, right on!"

north kern state prison

'beautiful dark bb

— silver

— 'please don't
pick up
hitch-hikers' sign

"We have a no-hostage policy, which means we can't exchange for you if you're taken." With these words, and after giving me a whistle, Lt. Ronald Hansen ushers me past the lethal electric fence and into the yard. I'm a bit nervous. Inside, inmates with tattoos stroll around a playing field or play checkers. In "A" Block, three men share a shower. Lt. Hansen wakes an inmate to show me his cell. We visit the dining hall and look at the menu. Lt. Hansen, a round man with a

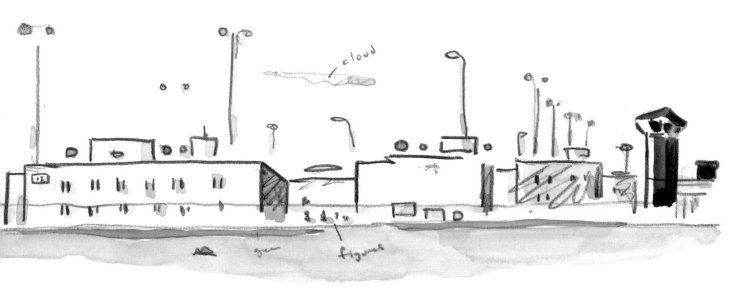

cloud

gras

figures

hands
behind
backs

red tie, has lost 58 pounds in the last nine months and is greeted by coworkers with comments like, "You're going to blow away!" Guards are cheerful. I start to relax. The cost of keeping one inmate is over $25,000 a year. On the way out I come across a busload of new arrivals. They stand in line, arms behind back (the prison rule). Most will return. Most are my age.

harlan ranch

At six in the morning the sun is an inch off the horizon and Greg Harlan is branding a calf. Seventy head of eight-month-old Brangus (Brahman and Angus cross) crash the metal chute and wait their turn. Harlan's ranch hands clamp tags through calves' ears and jab vaccine shots (for red water and blackleg) while Harlan brands, gently rolling the hot iron into the flesh for a clean mark. The five-hundred-pound calves go to their knees, spit, bellow. The brand is in the shape of a spear and has been in the family five generations. Harlan tells me the ranch's history in Fresno County back to 1848 then lets me brand a calf. Smoke rises from its back. At eight o'clock the last calf is branded. Just before it bursts out the chute, Harlan rubs its forehead.

bee biology facility

Kim Fondrk artificially inseminates anesthetized queen bees. That's just one of the things he does as a research aid at the facility. He also sticks numbered tags on bees so they can be monitored in the indoor glass hive. Fondrk points out the tagged queen with all the surrounding bees "groomin' her and lickin' her and feedin' her." Sounds like the life. Gesturing outside to other hives he asks, "Wanna open one up?" So we pull on veils, light a smoker, walk out, and crack a hive – revealing wood frames caked with bees and dripping with honey. The smoke calms the bees. Fondrk starts telling me about nectar, wax, pollen. "Well, I just got stung," he says. He continues, talking about drones, virgin queens, and the dancing bee whose wild circular spinning directs other bees to food. Do bees ever get stuck in his beard? "Yeah, then you can flick 'em out, or kill 'em. Mainly kill 'em." He chuckles, "It's you or them."

the capitol building

"Hi Josh." "Hi Josh." "Hi Josh." Everybody in the halls of the Capitol knows Josh Pane because Josh Pane, lobbyist, is the *man*. I tag along as he points out who's who among other lobbyists: "He's against us," "He's working it." Pane (pronounced like the Italian bread) is lobbying for a Native American gambling bill. There are all sorts of special interests: casinos, tribes, unions, the governor. Pane's clients today, two members of the Palm Springs Agua Caliente Tribal Council, tag along too, working cell phones and passing out cards. We take a meeting in an assemblyman's office. We visit the Senate gallery. We visit the Assembly gallery. Pane picks up five messages from his cell phone. The bill shifts from the rules committee to the floor. It's hard to know what will happen and Pane says there's a pool betting on when it will end.

donner ski ranch

Snowboarders swoop gracefully down the mountain, torque their bodies far out with centrifugal force, mock gravity. Sometimes gravity mocks back. Sierra Brown sits in a snowbank and lets me in on the finer points of the face plant. You lose an edge, flip, plant. When it's really bad you call it a "yard sale" because you "lose all your gear." Brown hasn't crashed today. She's a junior in high school and wears

plum lipstick. As she packs a snowball she tells me the advantage of snowboarding being *the* trend: "Like if you say 'I went snowboarding' it's like, 'oh, cool!' Blah, blah, blah." Nobody skis, everyone boards. Gear is important. So are guys. Guys are gear too in a way, but cooler. All the hot young guys board. A runaway board shoots by. Yard sale.

enloe medical center

The boy is six pounds fourteen ounces, twenty inches long, twenty-two hours old. He makes small noises and keeps his eyes closed. He rests on his mother in the maternity ward – breathing, their bodies rise and fall together. As the mother breast-feeds she tells me, "It kinda hurt at first but he's learned to do it better." The boy sucks his own fist: "Nothing's going to come out of that!" A doctor comes in to check on things and thumps the boy with a stethoscope. The boy cries. Desperate, body-shaking cries, muffled finally by a nipple.

prairie creek redwoods state park

This is what Joy Oilar, mill worker wife, thinks of protesters: "They urinate in my front yard. Leaking cars, oil spots. Huge mess to clean up. Trash everywhere . . . If they want to get their point across they need to look presentable. I understand their point of view, but they need to understand the amount of jobs. My grandfather was a choker setter, uncles are loggers, brother works for the sawmill. We value these trees as much as they do. We live here."

This is what Maya Watts, protester, thinks of loggers: "A lot of loggers agree with us to some extent. But they get in trouble talking with us. We've been chased by loggers. They're bigger than us. Loggers, or loggers' wives, or loggers' husbands I guess if there are those, if they cut down the forest they're not going to have jobs. [A barefoot girl walks up and gives me a frog.] We got trees. We got love. We got smiles. If it saves a tree it's totally worth it."

eureka fire department

Fire Chief John McFarland spent the day practicing for a tsunami but it's quiet now and late at night and raining so he shows me around. His office has toy fire trucks. Upstairs has a kitchen, Ping-Pong and pool tables, three firemen in front of a TV. We go downstairs to the truck (but don't use the fire pole). Boots with pants and suspenders already attached, called turnouts, wait at the doors. "If the bell rings, [firemen] kick off their shoes, jump in their boots, and they're off," says McFarland. He lets me sit in the driver's seat. The truck has compartments for oxygen canisters, flashlights, hoses, ropes. "Rappeling. We can go ten stories. That's always fun." He hands me a plastic bag with a stuffed teddy bear inside. "You can get a kid to stop crying in seconds. Every fire vehicle carries a bear. And they work."

russian gulch

After pulling on pink waterproof socks and stretching into a weathered wet suit, Mike Higgins makes a mental checklist. He looks around: "Oh, paddle!" We leave his VW van and head to the beach. The kayak gets momentarily stuck in bushes. Higgins is kayaking the California coast, writing and taking photos for his elaborate website – www.kayaker.net. He lives in Cazadero, his favorite coastline is around Mendocino. He tells me why he loves kayaking: "It's getting to see places that, where did my seat go? You travel out to coves and it's right in my backyard." Higgins finds his seat and then, with a final push, takes to the ocean. On the water he's graceful.

united farm workers

 "Chava" Salvador Mendoza straddles a chair. The office has a painting of César Chávez, a photo of Chava at a picket line wearing a cowboy hat. Now he wears a baseball hat and talks with me about the harvest through interpreter Gilberto Rodriguez (who talks through a curvy mustache). Grapes, cut from vines, thrown on trays, loaded behind the tractor: hard work for not much. *"Trabajo* difficult. *Sí."* Chava

worked for twenty years in the vineyards before becoming an organizer. "I already went through this. Saw a lot of suffering." He goes outside and gives forty bucks to a union employee whose car broke down. He comes back and talks about workers' difficulties, the company, benefits, his plan to make workers see the union's way. Does Chava drink wine? "*Sí*. We only drink wine that's under contract."

industrial light & magic

Picture this: in an indistinguishable building not so far far away from other indistinguishable buildings, Nagisa Yamamoto is bouncing down a dark hallway, the top of her highlighted hair barely coming up to the navel of a nearby statue of Darth Vader.

Yamamoto is trendy, very friendly. She has stripes on her pants, an animated smile. She flies me by toy-covered monitors showing graphics, machetes, explosions, and tells me that one second of new film can take days of work. The company is finishing work on the next Star Wars movie.

She takes me to a screening room with R2D2, a model shop with an "EYES" drawer, the art department. She swears me to secrecy. Then Yamamoto blows through a door and we come face-to-face with a Battle Droid.

tomales bay oyster company

"It's an ugly oyster," says Drew Alden, holding up the offending mollusk. He hands me another. "This is much nicer. This is a nice, deep-cupped, pretty oyster. Nice tight little nugget." An oyster's good looks are determined by how it's grown. Alden himself has sunburned skin and wavy gray hair and owns the company. He begins sentences with phrases like "the thrill of farming" but is a bit tired as he harvested at one a.m. last night (he used to go to bars, then harvest, but now has a kid). We drive to town in his truck to pick up some coffee and Alden gives me the science. It's all about lunar cycles and over my head though it sounds really cool. Back on the docks there's a cat ("He's an oyster-eater.") and the harvest. Oysters are washed, sorted in bubbling tanks. They grow in mesh socks tied to pipes in the bay. There are twenty-six miles of pipe, 900,000 oysters – it's a small farm. They have a barge named *Gladys*.

the new superfish

Two humpbacks roll through the water. One is a calf. It sticks its fluke in the air and plays upside down. "That's calf behavior right there!" shouts naturalist Susan Sherman from the deck of our boat. She wears binoculars and rubber boots and holds a foot-long plastic model of a humpback. The humpbacks in the water are eighty feet long: beautiful, slow, huge. We see only a wheeling part: blowhole, dorsal fin, dappled

surrounded
by porpoise,
sea lions

white fluke. Then they're gone. We wait on board *The New Superfish*. The whales surface, blow a pungent smell. "Humpback whales have terrible breath," says Sherman. "Man, they have the worst breath. Ha ha!" They dive, leave spots of flat water. People on board crowd the gunwale. And when the whales come up on the other side of the boat it makes me wonder who's checking out whom.

south beach

Clouds scud the horizon, the light grows soft, and the moon comes out. It's a beautiful place. I jump in the waves, quickly, then stand at the edge of the ocean. And I wonder, did Jay Snow make it? Did he walk straight into the Pacific like he said he would? "I'm never going to stop walking, that's just the way it's going to be." I start thinking about Jim Brunberg playing his mandolin, Lilly Poon playing mahjong, and

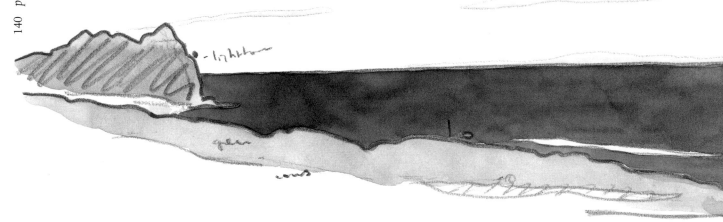

Julie Beddome driving her purple Yahoo! car. I think about Funk Doobiest on the mike, Alfredo Castillejo and his leaf blower, Matt Hall and his "yumbas," Sierra Brown and her snowboard. Waves crash into sand: Maya Watts, Nagisa Yamamoto, Chava Mendoza. The waves sound like Taiko drums, elephant seals, ravers. And for me, all of them, all of them, make California.